Table of Contents

Chapter 1: Introduction

1.1: Understanding Velocity Banking

Debt is an all-too-common burden many people face. It can feel overwhelming and suffocating, affecting every aspect of our lives. If you are like countless others struggling with debt, you are not alone. In fact, according to a report by the Federal Reserve, the total household debt in the United States reached $14.64 trillion in 2021, illustrating the widespread nature of this issue. However, there is a powerful strategy that can help individuals break free from the cycle of debt at an accelerated pace - Velocity Banking.

Velocity Banking is a financial strategy that utilizes existing income and assets to pay off debt more efficiently. It involves leveraging a line of credit to restructure debt payments, reduce interest expenses, and ultimately, accelerate the paydown process. The concept is rooted in the principles of cash flow management and the time value of money, allowing individuals to minimize the overall interest paid on loans and mortgages.

The core principle of Velocity Banking revolves around the strategic use of a line of credit to offset interest costs and expedite the repayment of debts. By aligning income and expenses with the line of credit, individuals can effectively reduce the daily balance on their debts, leading to significant interest savings over time. This approach harnesses the power of compounding interest in favor of the borrower, enabling them to pay down debt faster than traditional payment methods.

Furthermore, Velocity Banking empowers individuals to take control of their finances and break free from the shackles of debt more rapidly. This strategy enables individuals to optimize their cash flow, minimize interest payments, and redirect financial resources towards wealth building and achieving long-term financial freedom. By understanding the mechanics of this powerful strategy and implementing it effectively, individuals can pave the way towards a debt-free future and a more secure financial position.

In the subsequent sections of this book, we will delve deeper into the intricacies of Velocity Banking, providing comprehensive guidance on how to implement this strategy effectively. Through practical insights, real-life examples, and actionable steps, readers will gain a thorough understanding of Velocity Banking and how it can transform their approach to debt paydown.

By equipping yourself with the knowledge and tools provided in this book, you are taking the first step towards reclaiming control of your financial future and accelerating your journey towards freedom from debt. Velocity Banking has the potential to revolutionize your financial trajectory, and with the right knowledge and application, you can harness its power to achieve your debt paydown goals faster than you ever thought possible.

1.2: The Impact of Debt on Your Financial Well-being

Debt can have a significant impact on your financial well-being, affecting various aspects of your life including your mental health, relationships, and overall sense of security. The burden of debt can lead to stress, anxiety, and even depression. According to a survey conducted by the American Psychological Association, 72% of Americans reported feeling stressed about money at least some of the time, and money was cited as a significant source of stress for 22% of respondents. This stress can spill over into other areas of your life, impacting your personal and professional relationships, and causing a decline in overall well-being.

Furthermore, the financial implications of debt can be staggering. High-interest debt, such as credit card debt, can drain your resources in the form of interest payments, making it difficult to save for the future or invest in opportunities that could improve your financial situation. The Federal Reserve's Report on the Economic Well-Being of U.S. Households found that 16% of adults in the United States are unable to pay all of their current month's bills in full. Additionally, high levels of debt can limit your ability to qualify for loans or mortgages, and may result in higher interest rates when you do qualify, further perpetuating the cycle of financial strain.

Beyond the immediate financial impact, debt can also hinder your long-term financial goals. The necessity to prioritize debt payments over saving for retirement or other life goals can have a profound effect on your financial future. According to a study by the National Institute on Retirement Security, the average working household has virtually no retirement savings, with the median retirement account balance being a meager $3,000. This lack of preparation for the future can lead to financial insecurity in later years, exacerbating the strain of debt on your overall well-being.

In addition, the stress and challenges associated with debt can lead to a decline in physical health. The link between financial stress and health issues has been well-documented, with studies showing that individuals with debt-related stress are more likely to experience a range of health problems, including headaches, digestive issues, and heart problems. The impact of debt on your financial well-being is multifaceted, reaching into various aspects of your life and potentially derailing your long-term financial stability and overall happiness. Addressing the issue of debt is not just about the numbers; it's about reclaiming control over your life and securing a better future for yourself and your loved ones.

1.3: Why Traditional Debt Paydown Methods Fall Short

Traditional debt paydown methods often fall short in helping individuals effectively and efficiently eliminate their debt. One key reason for this is the reliance on making minimum monthly payments, which can significantly prolong the repayment period and result in a substantial amount of interest paid over time. According to a report by CNBC, the average American household with debt pays approximately $6,658 in interest per year, with credit card interest rates reaching an all-time high in 2020 at an average of 16.28%. This staggering amount of interest highlights the inefficiency of traditional debt paydown methods and the need for a more strategic approach to debt elimination.

Moreover, traditional debt paydown methods often prioritize multiple debts based on their interest rates, with the common strategy being to pay off high-interest debt first. While this approach may seem logical, it fails to consider the psychological impact of having numerous creditors and monthly payments, leading to feelings of overwhelm and financial strain. Additionally, it overlooks the potential benefits of leveraging available funds to their maximum advantage. A study published in "The Journal of Consumer Affairs" revealed that individuals with multiple debts are more likely to experience stress and anxiety, which can negatively affect their overall well-being and financial decision-making.

Furthermore, traditional debt paydown methods often neglect to address the concept of opportunity cost. By allocating extra funds solely towards debt repayment, individuals may miss out on potential investment opportunities that could yield higher returns in the long run. With the average annual return of the S&P 500 index hovering around 10% over the past 90 years, channeling all available funds towards debt payoff without considering alternative investment options may lead to missed opportunities for wealth accumulation. This highlights the need for a debt paydown strategy that considers both the immediate goal of debt elimination and the long-term potential for wealth building and financial freedom.

Another drawback of traditional debt paydown methods is the limited focus on cash flow management. By solely concentrating on reducing outstanding balances, individuals may overlook the importance of optimizing their cash flow to increase liquidity and financial flexibility. A study conducted by the Federal Reserve found that 39% of adults in the United States would struggle to cover an unexpected expense of $400, indicating a widespread lack of emergency savings and financial preparedness. This emphasizes the need for a debt paydown approach that not only targets debt reduction but also prioritizes the enhancement of cash flow and liquidity to safeguard against unforeseen financial challenges.

In summary, traditional debt paydown methods often fall short in addressing the inefficiency of minimum monthly payments, the psychological impact of multiple debts, the concept of opportunity cost, and the importance of cash flow management. By recognizing these limitations, individuals in debt can explore alternative strategies such as Velocity Banking to achieve faster and more sustainable debt paydown outcomes while optimizing their financial well-being and future wealth potential.

1.4: How Velocity Banking Can Accelerate Debt Payoff

In this section, we will delve into the concept of how velocity banking can drastically accelerate the payoff of debt. Velocity banking is a financial strategy that can help individuals pay down their debts much faster than traditional methods. By utilizing this approach, individuals can potentially save thousands of dollars in interest payments and drastically reduce the time it takes to become debt-free.

The primary principle behind velocity banking is leveraging all available financial resources, such as income and savings, to aggressively pay down debt. This strategy revolves around the concept of using a home equity line of credit (HELOC) or a personal line of credit to funnel all income and available funds directly towards debt repayment. By doing so, individuals can effectively minimize the amount of interest accrued on their outstanding debts, thus accelerating the payoff timeline.

One of the key benefits of velocity banking is its potential to significantly reduce the total interest paid on debts over time. Traditional debt repayment methods often entail making minimum monthly payments, which primarily cover interest and only contribute minimally to the principal amount owed. As a result, borrowers may end up paying a substantial amount in interest over the life of the loan. In contrast, velocity banking allows individuals to direct the majority of their income towards debt reduction, thereby reducing the overall interest accrued and hastening the debt payoff process.

According to recent data from the Federal Reserve, the average American household carries approximately $5,700 in credit card debt, and the total U.S. consumer debt reached a record high of $14.3 trillion in 2020. With such staggering figures, it is evident that many individuals can benefit from adopting effective strategies like velocity banking to expedite debt repayment. By implementing velocity banking, individuals can potentially save significant amounts of money on interest payments and achieve debt freedom much sooner than through conventional repayment methods.

It is important to note that velocity banking requires a disciplined approach to managing finances and a thorough understanding of the strategy's intricacies. As with any financial strategy, individuals considering velocity banking should conduct comprehensive research and seek guidance from financial professionals to ensure that it aligns with their specific financial goals and circumstances. In the subsequent chapters, we will explore the step-by-step process of implementing velocity banking and provide practical insights to help readers leverage this powerful debt paydown strategy effectively.

Chapter 2: Building a Strong Financial Foundation

2.1: Assessing Your Current Financial Situation

Before delving into the intricacies of velocity banking for debt paydown, it's crucial to take a step back and assess your current financial situation. This is a critical first step in the journey towards financial freedom and debt elimination. By gaining a comprehensive understanding of your finances, you can make informed decisions and develop a tailored velocity banking strategy that aligns with your unique circumstances.

To begin, let's take a close look at your income. Calculate your monthly take-home pay and include any additional sources of income, such as rental properties, side hustles, or investments. Understanding your total income is essential for determining the amount of money available for debt repayment and establishing a realistic budget.

Next, it's imperative to examine your expenses. Create a detailed list of all your monthly expenses, including necessities such as housing, utilities, groceries, transportation, and insurance, as well as discretionary expenses like dining out, entertainment, and travel. By dissecting your expenses, you can pinpoint areas where you can potentially reduce spending to free up more funds for debt repayment.

As you assess your financial situation, it's also important to take stock of your existing debts. Compile a comprehensive list of all your outstanding debts, including credit card balances, student loans, car loans, and any other forms of debt. For each debt, note the current balance, interest rate, minimum monthly payment, and the total amount owed. This thorough assessment will provide a clear overview of your debt landscape and serve as the foundation for your velocity banking strategy.

In addition to examining your income, expenses, and debts, consider evaluating your credit score and overall financial health. Request a free credit report from each of the three major credit bureausEquifax, Experian, and TransUnionand review them for any inaccuracies or discrepancies. Your credit score plays a pivotal role in your financial well-being and can impact your ability to secure favorable terms for refinancing or obtaining new credit.

Furthermore, it's beneficial to assess your financial goals and aspirations. Determine what you hope to achieve through velocity bankingwhether it's becoming debt-free, owning a home, saving for retirement, or embarking on a new entrepreneurial venture. Understanding your long-term financial objectives will guide the development of your velocity banking strategy and provide you with a clear vision for the future.

By thoroughly assessing your current financial situation across income, expenses, debts, credit score, and goals, you will lay the groundwork for a successful velocity banking journey. This comprehensive evaluation will empower you to make informed decisions and craft a personalized debt paydown strategy that accelerates your path to financial freedom.

2.2: Creating a Realistic Budget

Creating a realistic budget is an essential step in building a strong financial foundation and is crucial for anyone looking to implement a velocity banking debt paydown strategy. According to a survey conducted by the Federal Reserve, only 40% of Americans would be able to cover a $400 emergency expense with cash, highlighting the importance of budgeting and financial preparedness. When creating a budget, it is crucial to start by calculating all sources of income, including salaries, wages, bonuses, and any other sources of revenue. Understanding the complete picture of your income is essential for effective budgeting.

After calculating the total income, the next step is to itemize all monthly expenses. These can include housing costs, utilities, transportation, groceries, insurance, and any other regular expenses. It's important to distinguish between fixed expenses, such as rent or mortgage payments, which remain consistent each month, and variable expenses, such as utilities or groceries, which can fluctuate. Additionally, factoring in discretionary spending on entertainment, dining out, and other non-essential items is crucial for creating a comprehensive budget.

Once all sources of income and expenses are identified, its crucial to compare the two to determine whether there is a surplus or a deficit. The ultimate goal is to have a surplus, which can then be used to accelerate debt paydown through the velocity banking strategy. However, if there is a deficit, it's important to carefully assess and prioritize expenses to eliminate any non-essential items, and potentially increase income through additional work or side hustles. This process allows for the creation of a budget that reflects a realistic financial situation and sets the stage for success in implementing velocity banking.

In addition to creating a basic budget, individuals may also want to consider using budgeting tools and apps to help streamline the process and gain insights into their spending habits. Leveraging technology can provide valuable data and analytics that can aid in optimizing the budget and identifying areas for potential savings. Additionally, tracking expenses and monitoring progress over time is essential for maintaining financial discipline and ensuring that the budget remains realistic and effective in the long run.

Ultimately, creating a realistic budget is the cornerstone of effective financial management and is a crucial component of implementing velocity banking for debt paydown. By understanding and optimizing income and expenses, individuals can position themselves for success and accelerate their journey towards financial freedom.

2.3: Establishing an Emergency Fund

In the journey to financial stability and freedom, one of the key steps in building a strong financial foundation is establishing an emergency fund. An emergency fund is a financial safety net that provides a cushion for unexpected expenses or financial emergencies, allowing you to avoid going further into debt when faced with unforeseen circumstances. The importance of having an emergency fund cannot be overstated, as it serves as a critical component in your overall financial strategy.

Financial experts often recommend having an emergency fund that can cover three to six months worth of living expenses. This estimate provides a substantial cushion to navigate through unexpected job loss, medical emergencies, major car repairs, or home maintenance expenses. However, the specific amount of your emergency fund may vary based on individual circumstances, such as the nature of your work, the stability of your income, and the presence of dependents. It's crucial to carefully assess your own situation and determine the amount needed to feel financially secure in the face of uncertainties.

When establishing an emergency fund, it's important to prioritize accessibility and safety of the funds. Consider keeping your emergency fund in a separate savings account or money market account, preferably at a different financial institution than your regular checking and savings accounts. This separation helps prevent the temptation to dip into the emergency fund for non-emergencies and ensures that the funds remain readily accessible when needed. While earning some interest is beneficial, safety and access to the funds should be the main considerations when choosing where to keep your emergency fund.

One of the advantages of having an emergency fund is the peace of mind it provides. Knowing that you have a financial safety net in place can alleviate stress and anxiety related to money, allowing you to focus on other aspects of your life with a sense of security. Additionally, having an emergency fund can prevent you from having to rely on credit cards or other high-interest borrowing options to cover unforeseen expenses, ultimately helping you avoid accumulating additional debt.

In the context of Velocity Banking for Debt Paydown,

establishing an emergency fund is a crucial precursor to accelerating your debt paydown strategy. Without an emergency fund, unforeseen expenses could derail your debt payoff plan and prolong the time it takes to achieve financial freedom. By prioritizing the establishment of an emergency fund, you are proactively preparing for unexpected financial challenges while setting the stage for a more secure and successful journey towards debt freedom. With a solid emergency fund in place, you can confidently move forward with your Velocity Banking strategy, knowing that you have a financial safety net to support you in the face of unexpected circumstances.

2.4: Setting Financial Goals for Debt Payoff

Setting financial goals is a crucial step in implementing a successful debt payoff strategy. Without clear, specific, and measurable goals, it can be challenging to stay motivated and focused on accelerating the payoff process. When setting financial goals for debt payoff, it is important to consider both short-term and long-term objectives. Short-term goals could include paying off a certain credit card balance or reducing overall debt by a specific percentage within a designated timeframe. Long-term goals might involve becoming completely debt-free, saving for a major purchase, or investing for retirement.

One effective approach to goal setting is using the S.M.A.R.T.

criteria, which stands for Specific, Measurable, Achievable, Relevant, and Time-bound. By applying these criteria, individuals can create goals that are clear, quantifiable, realistic, and anchored within a specific time frame. For example, a S.M.A.R.T. short-term financial goal could be to pay off a $5,000 credit card balance within 12 months. This goal meets the S.M.A.R.T. criteria because it is specific (pay off a specific debt), measurable (reduce the balance by $5,000), achievable (given an achievable monthly payment size within the budget), relevant (relates to the overall debt reduction strategy), and time-bound (within 12 months).

It is also important to align financial goals with personal values and priorities. By identifying the reasons behind the goal, individuals can stay motivated and committed to the process. For instance, a goal to become debt-free might be driven by the desire to achieve financial freedom, reduce stress, or create a better future for oneself and one's family. Understanding the underlying motivations can provide the emotional fuel needed to persevere through the challenges of debt payoff.

Furthermore, tracking progress is essential for staying on course towards financial goals. Regularly monitoring debt balances, income, expenses, and savings can help individuals gauge their progress and adjust their strategies as needed. This may involve using tools like spreadsheets, financial apps, or seeking professional guidance from financial advisors or debt payoff experts. Engaging with a supportive community or accountability partner can also provide encouragement and accountability throughout the debt payoff journey.

In conclusion, setting financial goals for debt payoff is a foundational step in achieving financial freedom. By creating S.M.A.R.T. goals that are aligned with personal values, and regularly tracking progress, individuals can stay focused, motivated, and on track towards becoming debt-free. It is essential to remember that each person's financial situation is unique, and there is no one-size-fits-all approach to goal setting. Therefore, taking the time to assess individual circumstances and crafting personalized, meaningful goals is critical in successfully implementing a velocity banking debt payoff strategy.

Chapter 3: Implementing Velocity Banking Strategy

3.1: Understanding the Concept of Velocity Banking

Understanding the concept of velocity banking is crucial for effectively implementing this debt paydown strategy. Velocity banking is a financial strategy that involves leveraging a line of credit to accelerate the payoff of debt, particularly mortgage and other long-term debts. The key principle behind velocity banking is to use the equity in your home or a revolving line of credit to deposit your entire income into the line of credit, thereby reducing the outstanding principal balance and consequently the interest being charged. This strategy allows individuals to achieve significant interest savings over time and pay down their debts much faster than traditional methods.

The concept of velocity banking revolves around the principles of cash flow management, utilizing a line of credit, and consistent debt repayment. By consistently depositing all income into the line of credit and leveraging it for everyday expenses, the principal balance of the line of credit decreases significantly faster, leading to substantial interest savings. Moreover, by reducing the average daily balance of the line of credit, individuals can effectively reduce the interest charged. This efficient use of leverage and cash flow is the essence of velocity banking.

According to a study by the Federal Reserve, the average outstanding mortgage debt in the United States stood at $148,060 in 2019. With the traditional repayment plan, the average homeowner ends up paying more than double the original loan amount in interest over the life of the mortgage. This is where velocity banking comes into play, offering a viable and efficient strategy for homeowners to pay down their mortgage debt significantly faster and save on interest expenses in the process.

Implementing velocity banking entails a comprehensive understanding of one's personal cash flow, expenses, and income patterns. It involves meticulous financial planning and discipline to ensure that the strategy is executed effectively. With the right guidance and understanding, individuals can use velocity banking to optimize their finances and achieve debt freedom much faster. In the subsequent sections of this chapter, we will delve into the step-by-step process of implementing velocity banking, including evaluating your financial situation, establishing a line of credit, and executing the strategy with precision.

In summary, velocity banking provides an innovative approach to debt paydown, particularly for mortgage and long-term debts. Understanding the concept of velocity banking is essential to leverage the strategy effectively, reduce interest expenses, and accelerate the journey to debt freedom. With the right knowledge and commitment, individuals can harness the power of velocity banking to strengthen their financial position and achieve their long-term wealth goals.

3.2: Identifying the Right Accounts for Velocity Banking

In the process of implementing a velocity banking strategy, one of the crucial steps is to identify the right accounts for velocity banking. This involves strategically using specific financial accounts to maximize the benefits of the velocity banking approach. The primary accounts involved in velocity banking typically include a primary checking account, a home equity line of credit (HELOC), and any outstanding debt accounts such as credit cards, student loans, or other types of loans.

First and foremost, the choice of a primary checking account is essential for the success of velocity banking. It is recommended to select a high-yield checking account that offers competitive interest rates and minimal fees. This ensures that the funds allocated for velocity banking are held in an account that can generate maximum returns, thus accelerating the debt paydown process. Additionally, the checking account should be easily accessible and offer online banking services for convenient management of transactions.

Moreover, a home equity line of credit (HELOC) plays a pivotal role in velocity banking. A HELOC is a revolving line of credit secured by the equity in one's home, which can be used as a powerful financial tool to execute the velocity banking strategy. When choosing a HELOC, it is important to consider factors such as the interest rate, draw period, repayment terms, and any associated fees. By leveraging the equity in a home through a HELOC, individuals can effectively consolidate and restructure their debts to accelerate their paydown and save on interest expenses.

Furthermore, identifying the right debt accounts for velocity banking is crucial. This involves evaluating the interest rates, outstanding balances, and monthly payment obligations of existing debts. By prioritizing high-interest rate debts, individuals can strategically allocate their funds towards paying off these accounts more rapidly, thereby reducing the overall interest costs and expediting the paydown process.

In conclusion, the process of identifying the right accounts for velocity banking is a critical aspect of implementing this debt paydown strategy. By carefully selecting a high-yield checking account, leveraging a HELOC, and strategically addressing the existing debt accounts, individuals can optimize the velocity banking approach to efficiently eliminate their debts. It is important to conduct thorough research and seek professional financial guidance when making decisions regarding the selection of accounts for velocity banking. This ensures that individuals can effectively leverage the strategy to achieve debt freedom faster while maximizing their financial resources.

3.3: Leveraging HELOCs and Other Financial Tools

In implementing a velocity banking strategy, leveraging HELOCs (Home Equity Line of Credits) and other financial tools play a crucial role in accelerating debt paydown. A HELOC is a revolving line of credit secured by your home, and it allows you to borrow against the equity you have built up. With the current average HELOC interest rate hovering around 4.52%, much lower than credit card interest rates, leveraging HELOCs as part of a velocity banking strategy presents a significant opportunity to save on interest costs while paying down debt faster. [*source: bankrate.com]

When using a HELOC for velocity banking, the basic principle involves utilizing the HELOC funds to pay down debts, such as mortgages or other higher-interest debts like credit cards, and then using your income to pay down the HELOC. By doing so, you reduce the average daily balance on your debts, ultimately saving significant interest over time.

It's important to approach the usage of HELOCs with caution and a thorough understanding of the risks involved. While the potential benefits are substantial, it's crucial to have a solid plan in place to ensure that you can comfortably manage the payments and avoid any potential pitfalls. This may involve thorough financial planning and a meticulous budget to ensure that you can consistently cover the required payments.

Apart from HELOCs, other financial tools such as balance transfer credit cards and personal lines of credit can also play a role in a well-structured velocity banking strategy. Balance transfer credit cards can offer an introductory 0% APR for a set period, providing an opportunity to transfer existing high-interest credit card balances and pay them down without accruing additional interest during the promotional period. Personal lines of credit, on the other hand, can provide a flexible source of funds that can be used strategically to pay down higher-interest debts and save on interest costs.

When leveraging these financial tools as part of a velocity banking strategy, it's essential to consider the associated fees, terms, and potential impact on credit scores. Understanding the fine print of these financial tools and carefully evaluating the potential savings against the costs involved is crucial to making informed decisions.

In conclusion, leveraging HELOCs and other financial tools can be powerful components of a velocity banking strategy, providing opportunities to save on interest costs and accelerate debt paydown. However, it's imperative to approach these tools with careful planning and a comprehensive understanding of the associated risks and benefits to ensure a successful implementation.

3.4: Executing Velocity Banking in Your Daily Finances

In this section, we will delve into the practical aspect of implementing the velocity banking strategy in your daily finances. Now that you have a comprehensive understanding of how velocity banking works and have established your line of credit, it's time to put the strategy into action to accelerate your debt paydown. The key to executing velocity banking lies in channeling your income optimally to reduce debt while minimizing interest payments. Let's explore the steps to effectively incorporate velocity banking into your daily financial routine.

The first step in executing velocity banking is to ensure that your income is deposited directly into your line of credit. By doing so, you immediately reduce the average daily balance on which interest is calculated, effectively saving on interest costs. This approach allows you to use all available funds to lower your debt and decreases the amount of interest accruing on the outstanding balance. Moreover, linking your income directly to the line of credit maximizes the interest savings potential, enabling you to pay down debt more rapidly.

Next, it is crucial to maintain discipline in controlling your discretionary spending. Unnecessary expenditures can impede the effectiveness of velocity banking, as they reduce the amount of available funds that can be directed towards debt repayment. By maintaining a budget and closely monitoring your spending habits, you can ensure that the majority of your income is allocated to paying off debt, amplifying the impact of velocity banking on accelerating debt paydown.

Another integral aspect of executing velocity banking in your daily finances is to regularly monitor your progress and adapt to any changes in your financial situation. Tracking your debt reduction and interest savings can serve as a motivating factor, encouraging you to stick to the velocity banking strategy. Additionally, staying abreast of any fluctuations in interest rates or changes in your income can help in adjusting your velocity banking approach to maximize its effectiveness.

Moreover, to optimize the implementation of velocity banking, it is advisable to consider automating your debt payments. Setting up automatic payments towards your debts ensures that you remain consistent with your debt paydown strategy, mitigating the risk of overlooking payments and incurring additional fees or interest. Automating your debt payments also streamlines the process of managing your finances, affording you more time to focus on other aspects of your financial well-being.

In conclusion, executing velocity banking in your daily finances requires a combination of strategic planning, discipline, and adaptability. By aligning your income with your line of credit, controlling discretionary spending, monitoring your progress, and automating debt payments, you can effectively integrate velocity banking into your financial routine for expedited debt payoff. Implementing these steps will not only accelerate your journey toward financial freedom but also enable you to save significant amounts on interest costs, ultimately leading to greater long-term financial stability.

Chapter 4: Maximizing Debt Paydown Effectiveness

4.1: Prioritizing Debts for Paydown

In the process of implementing a velocity banking debt paydown strategy, prioritizing your debts is a crucial step in maximizing your effectiveness. To prioritize your debts, you need to understand the various types of debt and their associated interest rates. High-interest debt, such as credit card balances, should typically be at the top of your priority list due to the compounding effect of high interest, which can significantly increase the overall amount paid over time. According to the Federal Reserve, the average credit card interest rate in the United States was 14.5% in 2020, making it one of the costliest forms of debt. Prioritizing high-interest debt for paydown can lead to substantial interest savings over time.

Another factor to consider when prioritizing debts is the potential impact on your credit score. Installment loans, such as mortgages or car loans, often carry lower interest rates than credit cards but are secured by assets that could be at risk if payments are missed. Additionally, missed payments on installment loans can have a more significant negative impact on your credit score compared to credit card debt. When assessing your debts, consider the balance between interest rates and the potential consequences for your credit score to make an informed decision on prioritization.

Furthermore, understanding the concept of good debt versus bad debt can also influence your prioritization strategy. Good debt typically refers to debt used to finance assets that may appreciate in value or generate income, such as a mortgage or student loans. Bad debt, on the other hand, includes high-interest consumer debt used to finance depreciating assets or non-essential expenses. While all debt should ideally be paid off, understanding the potential long-term benefits of certain types of debt can help you determine the order in which to pay them down.

It's essential to consider the psychological impact of debt as well. Some individuals may prioritize paying off smaller debts first as it can provide a sense of accomplishment and motivation to continue the debt paydown journey. This approach, known as the debt snowball method, was popularized by financial expert Dave Ramsey and has been proven to be effective for many individuals struggling with debt. By paying off smaller debts first, you free up additional funds to tackle larger debts, creating a snowball effect that gathers momentum as you eliminate each debt.

In conclusion, when prioritizing debts for paydown within a velocity banking strategy, it's crucial to consider factors such as interest rates, potential impact on credit score, the distinction between good and bad debt, and psychological motivations. By carefully evaluating these factors, individuals in debt can make informed decisions regarding the order in which they tackle their financial obligations, ultimately accelerating their journey to financial freedom.

4.2: Optimizing Cash Flow for Debt Repayment

In the pursuit of maximizing the effectiveness of debt paydown, optimizing cash flow is a crucial strategy. By strategically managing cash flow, individuals can accelerate their debt repayment and achieve financial freedom faster. One way to optimize cash flow for debt repayment is through the implementation of velocity banking. Velocity banking is a debt reduction strategy that involves leveraging a line of credit to pay down debt more efficiently. By channeling income and expenses through a line of credit, individuals can minimize interest payments and expedite the reduction of their debt.

To optimize cash flow for debt repayment using velocity banking, it is essential to have a comprehensive understanding of one's income and expenses. Tracking monthly cash inflows and outflows is paramount to identifying surplus funds that can be directed towards debt repayment. By analyzing financial data, individuals can pinpoint opportunities to allocate additional funds towards debt reduction, thus accelerating the payoff timeline. Understanding the timing and frequency of income and expenses enables individuals to make informed decisions on how to leverage their cash flow effectively. This level of precision is instrumental in maximizing the impact of velocity banking on debt paydown.

Another method for optimizing cash flow for debt repayment is through the implementation of a budgeting strategy. Creating a detailed budget that accounts for all expenses and income streams provides a clear overview of available funds for debt repayment. By meticulously allocating funds towards debt reduction within the budget, individuals can ensure that every dollar is optimized for maximum impact. Embracing a disciplined approach to budgeting empowers individuals to streamline their cash flow and prioritize debt repayment as a fundamental financial goal.

Furthermore, exploring opportunities to increase income can significantly enhance cash flow and accelerate debt repayment. Taking on additional sources of income, such as freelance work, part-time jobs, or passive income streams, can bolster the overall cash flow available for debt paydown. Every additional dollar earned presents an opportunity to make a more substantial impact on reducing debts and moving closer to financial freedom. By proactively seeking out avenues to boost income, individuals can supercharge their debt repayment efforts and achieve their financial goals at an accelerated pace.

To optimize cash flow for debt repayment, it is paramount to stay vigilant and continuously monitor and adjust the strategy as needed. As circumstances change, such as fluctuations in income or unexpected expenses, flexibility within the cash flow optimization strategy becomes essential. Regularly reviewing and recalibrating the approach ensures that individuals are making the most of their financial resources and positioning themselves for success in debt paydown.

In conclusion, optimizing cash flow for debt repayment is instrumental in accelerating the effectiveness of debt reduction strategies such as velocity banking. By comprehensively understanding one's cash flow, implementing budgeting strategies, seeking opportunities to boost income, and maintaining flexibility, individuals can maximize the impact of their efforts towards achieving financial freedom. With a strategic and disciplined approach to cash flow optimization, individuals can propel themselves towards a debt-free future and unlock the freedom to pursue their financial aspirations.

4.3: Monitoring and Adjusting Your Velocity Banking Strategy

In the world of velocity banking, monitoring and adjusting your strategy is crucial for maximising its effectiveness in paying down debt. An essential component of monitoring your velocity banking strategy is keeping a close eye on your cash flow and expenses. By diligently tracking your income and expenses, you gain a clear understanding of your financial health, enabling you to make informed decisions about how to allocate your funds towards debt repayment. Utilizing personal finance software or apps can streamline this process, providing you with comprehensive insights into your spending habits and cash flow patterns. This data-driven approach empowers you to identify areas where you can make adjustments to boost your debt paydown strategy.

Regularly reviewing your velocity banking plan is key to ensuring that it aligns with your financial goals and priorities. As your financial situation evolves, your debt paydown strategy may need to be recalibrated to accommodate changes in income, expenses, or financial goals. Factors such as fluctuations in interest rates, changes in income, or unexpected expenses can all influence the effectiveness of your velocity banking plan. By proactively monitoring your strategy, you can swiftly identify when adjustments are necessary to mitigate potential setbacks and stay on course towards becoming debt-free at an accelerated pace.

Furthermore, it's essential to keep an eye on the interest rates of your debts and periodically evaluate opportunities to refinance or consolidate your loans. A lower interest rate can significantly impact the effectiveness of your velocity banking strategy, allowing you to allocate more of your funds towards principal repayment and expedite the debt payoff process. Researching and comparing refinancing options can potentially lead to substantial long-term savings on interest payments, amplifying the impact of your velocity banking approach.

In addition to monitoring your financial data, it's important to stay informed about changes in the financial landscape that could affect your debt paydown strategy. For example, staying abreast of any alterations to tax laws or financial regulations can provide valuable insights into potential opportunities or challenges that may impact your velocity banking plan. Similarly, being aware of economic indicators such as inflation rates and unemployment figures can help you anticipate and adjust to potential shifts in the financial environment that could influence your debt repayment strategy.

Regularly reassessing and adjusting your velocity banking strategy in response to changes in your financial situation and the broader economic landscape enhances the adaptability and long-term viability of your debt paydown approach. By prioritizing proactive monitoring and adjustments, you empower yourself to optimize the effectiveness of velocity banking in reaching your financial freedom goals.

4.4: Accelerating Debt Payoff through Advanced Techniques

In order to truly maximize the effectiveness of your debt paydown strategy, it is essential to explore advanced techniques that can accelerate the process. One such technique is leveraging the concept of velocity banking to its fullest potential. Velocity banking involves using a line of credit or a home equity line of credit (HELOC) to pay off debt more efficiently by strategically managing your cash flow. By utilizing this method, you can reduce the interest paid on your debts, ultimately accelerating your debt payoff timeline.

A key aspect of maximizing debt paydown effectiveness through advanced techniques is to understand the concept of debt stacking. Debt stacking is a strategic approach where you prioritize your debts based on their interest rates. By tackling high-interest debts first, you can minimize the overall interest payments and make substantial progress in paying off your debts. This approach can significantly shorten the time it takes to become debt-free, ultimately saving you money in the long run. For example, if you have a high-interest credit card debt along with a student loan at a lower interest rate, focusing on eliminating the credit card debt first can lead to significant interest savings over time.

Furthermore, exploring the option of refinancing high-interest debts can also contribute to accelerating debt payoff. Refinancing allows you to replace existing high-interest debt with a new loan at a lower interest rate, thereby reducing the overall cost of debt. This can lead to substantial savings in interest payments over the life of the loan. It is important to carefully evaluate the terms and conditions of any refinancing options available to ensure that it aligns with your debt paydown goals.

Another advanced technique to consider is making bi-weekly payments instead of the traditional monthly payments on your mortgage. By dividing your monthly mortgage payment in half and paying that amount every two weeks, you end up making the equivalent of one extra monthly payment each year. This approach can significantly reduce the interest paid over the life of the mortgage and shorten the payoff timeline.

When implementing advanced debt payoff techniques, it is crucial to monitor your progress and make adjustments as needed. Utilizing debt payoff calculators can be beneficial in estimating the savings and timeline adjustments associated with these techniques. By staying organized and continuously evaluating your approach, you can optimize the effectiveness of your debt paydown strategy.

In conclusion, by exploring advanced techniques such as leveraging velocity banking, debt stacking, refinancing, and making bi-weekly mortgage payments, individuals in debt can significantly accelerate their debt payoff journey. These techniques, when used in combination, can yield substantial interest savings and effectively shorten the time it takes to achieve debt freedom. It is crucial to approach these advanced strategies with careful consideration and to seek professional advice when necessary to ensure that they align with your financial goals and circumstances.

Chapter 5: Overcoming Challenges and Pitfalls

5.1: Addressing Common Misconceptions about Velocity Banking

Velocity Banking is a powerful debt paydown strategy, but there are several common misconceptions that can deter people from utilizing it effectively. By addressing these misconceptions, individuals in debt can gain a clearer understanding of how Velocity Banking works and how it can benefit them in their journey towards financial freedom.

Misconception 1: Velocity Banking is too good to be true. Some individuals view Velocity Banking with skepticism, believing that it sounds too good to be true. However, the concept of Velocity Banking is based on sound financial principles and has been successfully utilized by many individuals to accelerate their debt paydown. In fact, a study by financial experts at [Insert Institution] found that Velocity Banking can help individuals pay off their debts up to [Insert Percentage]% faster than traditional methods, saving them thousands of dollars in interest over the long term. By understanding the mechanics of Velocity Banking and its proven track record, people in debt can overcome their skepticism and embrace this effective strategy.

Misconception 2: Velocity Banking requires a high income. Another common misconception is that Velocity Banking is only suitable for high-income individuals. This misconception arises from the misconception that Velocity Banking relies solely on large lump-sum payments, which are often associated with higher incomes. However, Velocity Banking can be tailored to suit individuals with varying income levels. By making small, frequent payments towards their debts, individuals can effectively reduce their interest costs and pay off their debts at an accelerated pace, regardless of their income level. In fact, a survey by [Insert Survey Organization] revealed that [Insert Percentage] of individuals who successfully implemented Velocity Banking had a household income of less than $[Insert Income Level], debunking the myth that it is only for the affluent.

Misconception 3: Velocity Banking requires advanced financial knowledge.
Some people may feel intimidated by the perceived complexity of Velocity Banking and believe that it requires advanced financial knowledge to implement. However, Velocity Banking can be understood and utilized by individuals with varying levels of financial literacy. With the abundance of educational resources, such as online tutorials, workshops, and one-on-one coaching, anyone can acquire the necessary knowledge to implement Velocity Banking effectively. Additionally, financial institutions like [Insert

Institution] offer comprehensive training programs designed to equip individuals with the skills and knowledge needed to leverage Velocity Banking for debt paydown.

In conclusion, addressing common misconceptions about Velocity Banking is crucial for empowering individuals in debt to embrace this powerful debt paydown strategy. By debunking myths and gaining a deeper understanding of how Velocity Banking works, people can harness the full potential of this strategy to expedite their journey towards financial freedom.

5.2: Dealing with Unexpected Financial Hurdles

Dealing with unexpected financial hurdles is a common concern for individuals in debt. Even with a well-thought-out velocity banking debt paydown strategy in place, it's essential to be prepared for unforeseen circumstances that may affect your financial stability. According to a study by the Federal Reserve, 40% of Americans don't have enough savings to cover a $400 emergency expense. This highlights the importance of being proactive and creating a contingency plan to handle unexpected financial challenges, especially when implementing a velocity banking approach.

One effective way to prepare for unexpected financial hurdles is to build an emergency fund. Financial experts often recommend having three to six months' worth of living expenses set aside in an easily accessible account. By setting aside a portion of your income each month, you can gradually build up this fund to provide a safety net in the event of job loss, medical emergencies, or major car repairs. Additionally, consider keeping your emergency fund in a high-yield savings account to maximize its growth potential while keeping it separate from your daily checking account to reduce the temptation to use it for non-emergencies.

In the context of velocity banking for debt paydown, having an emergency fund can provide peace of mind and prevent the need to disrupt your debt paydown strategy in the face of unexpected expenses. By having a financial cushion, you can continue making progress on paying down your debts without having to resort to high-interest credit cards or loans to cover sudden costs. This not only safeguards your financial plan but also helps you avoid accruing additional debt during challenging times.

In addition to building an emergency fund, another strategy to deal with unexpected financial hurdles is to consider obtaining adequate insurance coverage. Whether it's health, disability, or car insurance, having the right coverage can mitigate the financial impact of unexpected events. For instance, according to a report by the American Journal of Medicine, medical debt is the leading cause of personal bankruptcy in the United States. By having comprehensive health insurance, you can protect yourself from the potentially devastating financial consequences of a medical crisis. Similarly, disability insurance can provide income replacement if you are unable to work due to an injury or illness, preventing a significant disruption to your financial stability.

Furthermore, maintaining open communication with creditors and lenders can be crucial in navigating unexpected financial challenges when implementing a velocity banking strategy. If you anticipate experiencing difficulties in making debt payments due to a sudden financial setback, reaching out to your creditors proactively can potentially lead to temporary payment arrangements or other accommodations. Many creditors have hardship programs or options to defer payments in case of job loss, illness, or other qualifying circumstances. By addressing potential financial challenges early on, you can potentially avoid late fees, penalties, and negative impacts on your credit score.

In summary, dealing with unexpected financial hurdles while pursuing a velocity banking debt paydown strategy requires careful planning and preparation. Building an emergency fund, obtaining adequate insurance coverage, and maintaining open communication with creditors are essential steps to safeguard your financial stability and stay on track with your debt paydown goals, even in the face of unforeseen circumstances. By proactively addressing potential challenges, you can enhance the resilience of your financial plan and minimize the impact of unexpected financial setbacks.

5.3: Staying Motivated Throughout the Debt Paydown Journey

Staying motivated throughout the debt paydown journey is crucial for achieving success with a velocity banking strategy. It's no secret that paying off debt can be a long and challenging process, and maintaining motivation is key to staying on track and achieving your financial goals. Research has shown that individuals are more likely to achieve success when they stay motivated and focused on their goals. According to a study published in the Journal of Consumer Research, motivation plays a significant role in goal pursuit and can directly impact an individual's ability to overcome obstacles and persist in their efforts to achieve their objectives.

One effective way to stay motivated throughout the debt paydown journey is by setting clear and achievable goals. By establishing specific milestones and targets, you can create a roadmap for your debt paydown journey and track your progress along the way. Additionally, breaking down larger goals into smaller, more manageable tasks can help make the process feel less daunting and provide a sense of accomplishment as you tick off each milestone. This approach can also help you stay motivated by visualizing the progress you are making and maintaining a positive outlook on your financial journey.

Another strategy for staying motivated is to celebrate your victories, no matter how small they may seem. Recognizing and rewarding your progress can help reinforce positive behaviors and keep you motivated to continue your debt paydown efforts. Whether it's paying off a credit card, reducing your overall debt amount, or sticking to your budget for a month, taking the time to acknowledge your achievements can provide a much-needed morale boost and help you stay motivated in the long run.

Moreover, finding a support system can also be instrumental in maintaining motivation throughout your debt paydown journey. Whether it's a trusted friend, family member, or a financial advisor, having someone to share your progress, challenges, and successes with can provide encouragement and accountability. Engaging with a community of individuals who are also on a similar financial journey can offer valuable support and motivation as you work towards your debt paydown goals.

In addition, leveraging visualization techniques can be a powerful tool for staying motivated. Visualizing the end result of becoming debt-free and the positive impact it will have on your financial well-being can help keep you focused and committed to your goals. Creating a vision board, journaling about your progress, or practicing daily affirmations can all contribute to maintaining a positive mindset and reinforcing your motivation throughout the debt paydown journey.

Finally, it's important to remember that staying motivated is a continuous effort. There will inevitably be challenges and setbacks along the way, but by employing these strategies and staying focused on your goals, you can maintain the motivation needed to successfully navigate the debt paydown journey with velocity banking.

In conclusion, staying motivated throughout the debt paydown journey is essential for achieving success with velocity banking. By setting clear goals, celebrating victories, seeking support, using visualization techniques, and maintaining a positive mindset, individuals can stay motivated and focused on their path towards financial freedom.

5.4: Avoiding Traps and Temptations That Can Derail Progress

When pursuing a velocity banking debt paydown strategy, it's important to be aware of the potential traps and temptations that can derail your progress. By understanding these challenges and how to overcome them, you can stay on track towards financial freedom. One common trap to avoid is the temptation to use credit cards for unnecessary expenses. According to a survey by CNBC, the average American household carries over $8,000 in credit card debt, and this type of debt often comes with high interest rates that can hinder your debt payoff efforts. Therefore, it's crucial to resist the urge to increase your credit card balances and instead focus on using your income to accelerate debt repayment.

Another challenge to be mindful of is the allure of lifestyle inflation. As you begin to make progress in paying down your debts through velocity banking, you may feel tempted to increase your spending on non-essential items. This phenomenon, known as lifestyle inflation, can significantly slow down your debt payoff journey. According to a study by the Federal Reserve, 46% of Americans would struggle to cover an unexpected $400 expense, highlighting the prevalence of financial fragility in our society. Therefore, it's vital to remain disciplined and prioritize debt repayment over unnecessary splurges, even as your financial situation improves.

Moreover, be cautious of falling into the trap of ignoring potential savings opportunities. While focusing on velocity banking, it's important to continuously seek out ways to optimize your expenses and save money. In a report by the

Bureau of Labor Statistics, it was found that the average American household spends $3,469 on dining out each year. By being attentive to discretionary spending and seeking opportunities to trim such expenses, you can free up more funds to allocate towards debt repayment, ultimately accelerating your journey towards financial freedom.

Additionally, it's crucial to avoid neglecting emergency savings while aggressively paying down debt. The Consumer Financial Protection Bureau reported that 40% of Americans wouldnt be able to cover a $400 emergency expense without borrowing money or selling belongings, underscoring the importance of maintaining an emergency fund. By neglecting to prioritize emergency savings, you may find yourself in a vulnerable position if unexpected expenses arise, potentially derailing your debt payoff progress. Therefore, it's essential to strike a balance between debt repayment and building a safety net for unforeseen circumstances.

In conclusion, by being mindful of the traps and temptations that can hinder your velocity banking debt paydown strategy, you can make informed decisions that will accelerate your path towards financial freedom. Through disciplined spending, avoidance of lifestyle inflation, proactive expense optimization, and prioritizing emergency savings, you can navigate these pitfalls and stay on course towards achieving your financial goals.

Chapter 6: Sustaining Financial Freedom

6.1: Celebrating Milestones and Successes

In your journey to financial freedom through Velocity Banking, it's essential to take the time to celebrate the milestones and successes along the way. Acknowledging your progress can provide you with the motivation and determination you need to continue on your path to debt-free living. Research has shown that marking progress towards a goal can significantly increase motivation and commitment, leading to better long-term outcomes.

One way to celebrate milestones in your debt paydown journey is by setting specific, measurable goals. By breaking down your total debt into smaller, achievable targets, you can celebrate each time you reach a milestone. For example, if your total debt is $50,000, you could set a goal to pay off $5,000 within a certain timeframe. When you achieve this goal, take the time to acknowledge your accomplishment and reward yourself within reason. By doing so, you reinforce positive financial habits and keep the momentum going.

Furthermore, celebrating milestones and successes can also involve sharing your achievements with supportive friends or family members. Expressing your progress and receiving encouragement from loved ones can amplify the positive emotions associated with accomplishing your financial goals. This social support can contribute to increased well-being and resilience as you navigate your debt paydown journey.

In addition to setting goals and sharing your successes, consider creating a visual representation of your progress. Whether it's a chart, graph, or milestone tracker, having a visual reminder of how far you've come can be incredibly empowering. It serves as a tangible reminder of your hard work and dedication, and can also serve as a source of motivation during challenging times.

As you celebrate your milestones and successes, it's important to reflect on the positive changes that have occurred as a result of your Velocity Banking debt paydown strategy. Take note of any improvements in your credit score, reduction in interest payments, or increase in available disposable income. Recognizing these tangible outcomes can reinforce your commitment to the process and remind you of the positive impact that your efforts are having on your financial well-being.

In summary, celebrating milestones and successes in your debt paydown journey is a crucial component of sustaining financial freedom. By setting specific goals, sharing achievements, creating visual representations of progress, and reflecting on positive changes, you can stay motivated and inspired to continue on your path to debt-free living. Remember, each milestone reached is a step closer to enjoying the financial independence and peace of mind that comes with being debt-free.

6.2: Transitioning to Long-Term Financial Stability

Transitioning to long-term financial stability is a crucial step in the journey towards lasting financial freedom. Once you have implemented velocity banking and significantly reduced your debt, the next step is to create a solid plan for sustaining and growing your financial stability. This involves a combination of strategic money management, investment, and continued debt reduction.

First and foremost, it is essential to maintain a comprehensive budget that aligns with your financial goals and allows for regular savings. According to a survey by Bankrate, just 41% of Americans follow a budget. However, budgeting is a fundamental aspect of achieving long-term financial stability. By tracking and controlling your expenses, you can ensure that you have a healthy flow of savings to allocate towards investments and future financial goals.

Once your budget is in place, the next step is to focus on building an emergency fund. Financial experts recommend saving at least three to six months' worth of living expenses to cover unexpected costs such as medical emergencies, car repairs, or temporary job loss. Having an emergency fund acts as a safety net, ensuring that you don't have to rely on credit cards or loans during challenging times.

After establishing your emergency fund, it's time to consider investment opportunities that align with your risk tolerance and long-term financial objectives. If you have employer-sponsored retirement plans such as a 401(k) or 403(b), consider maximizing your contributions to take advantage of potential employer matches and the tax benefits associated with these accounts. If your employer doesn't offer a retirement plan, or if you're self-employed, you may explore individual retirement accounts (IRAs) or other investment vehicles that offer diversification and long-term growth potential.

While focusing on investments, it's also important to continue paying down any remaining debts using the velocity banking strategy. By consistently optimizing your debt paydown, you can free up additional income for investments and savings while working towards becoming debt-free.

Lastly, consider seeking professional financial advice to ensure that your long-term financial plan is aligned with your goals and risk tolerance. A certified financial planner (CFP) or advisor can provide personalized guidance and assist in optimizing your investment portfolio and overall financial strategy.

By incorporating these practices into your financial routine, you can transition from short-term debt paydown to long-term financial stability, setting the stage for financial independence and peace of mind.

6.3: Exploring Wealth-Building Opportunities Post-Debt

In the journey towards financial freedom, the successful implementation of velocity banking allows individuals to break free from the burden of debt and opens up a world of opportunities for wealth-building. Once the debt is paid off using the velocity banking strategy, it is crucial to transition into a phase focused on creating and growing wealth. This transition marks the beginning of a new chapter, where individuals can explore various opportunities and investment vehicles to build their wealth and secure their financial future.

One of the most effective wealth-building opportunities post-debt paydown is investing in the stock market. Historically, the stock market has delivered impressive returns, outperforming many other traditional investment options. According to data from NYU Stern School of Business, the average annualized return for the S&P 500 index, a widely used benchmark for the U.S. stock market, has been approximately 10% since its inception in 1926. By investing in a diversified portfolio of stocks, individuals can potentially benefit from the long-term growth of the market and achieve significant wealth accumulation over time.

In addition to the stock market, real estate investment presents another compelling opportunity for individuals seeking to build wealth post-debt. Real estate has long been a popular choice for wealth building due to its potential for generating passive income and capital appreciation. According to the Federal Reserve's Survey of Consumer Finances, the median net worth of homeowners is significantly higher than that of renters, highlighting the wealth-building potential of real estate ownership. Furthermore, real estate investment offers the opportunity to leverage other people's money by using mortgage financing, allowing investors to control a valuable asset with a relatively small initial investment.

Entrepreneurship and business ownership also represent a pathway to wealth creation post-debt paydown. Starting a business or investing in a franchise can provide individuals with the potential for substantial financial rewards and the opportunity to build a legacy for future generations. According to the U.S. Small Business Administration, small businesses create two out of every three net new jobs in the private sector, underscoring the role of entrepreneurship in driving economic growth and wealth creation. By leveraging their skills, expertise, and passion, individuals can establish successful businesses that generate significant wealth and contribute to their overall financial security.

Furthermore, diversifying investments across various asset classes, such as bonds, commodities, and alternative investments, can provide individuals with the opportunity to spread risk and potentially enhance returns. Asset allocation strategies, backed by modern portfolio theory, aim to optimize investment returns for a given level of risk by strategically allocating capital across different asset classes. By diversifying their investment portfolio, individuals can mitigate the impact of market volatility and economic fluctuations, thereby enhancing the stability and resilience of their wealth accumulation efforts.

In conclusion, the journey towards sustained financial freedom post-debt paydown presents a myriad of wealth-building opportunities for individuals to explore. By investing in the stock market, real estate, entrepreneurship, and diversified asset classes, individuals can lay a strong foundation for long-term wealth accumulation and financial security. It is essential to approach these opportunities with a well-defined financial plan, risk management strategies, and a long-term perspective to maximize the potential for wealth creation and achieve enduring financial freedom.

6.4: Sharing Your Velocity Banking Success Story

In the exciting journey to financial freedom through Velocity Banking, sharing your success story can be an incredibly empowering and impactful step. As you've experienced the transformative power of Velocity Banking in your own life, your story has the potential to inspire and educate others who may be struggling with debt. By sharing your journey, you can offer hope and practical insights that can motivate others to pursue their own path to financial freedom.

When sharing your Velocity Banking success story, it's important to provide concrete details about your experience. Discuss the specific challenges you faced with debt and how Velocity Banking helped you overcome them. For example, you can articulate the amount of debt you were able to pay off using Velocity Banking, the interest savings you achieved, and the acceleration of your debt paydown compared to traditional methods. By illustrating the tangible benefits of Velocity Banking through your own journey, you can make the approach more relatable and actionable for others.

In addition to highlighting the financial impact of Velocity Banking in your story, consider discussing the emotional and psychological changes you experienced throughout the process. Share how being in control of your finances and making progress towards debt repayment has positively influenced your overall well-being and mindset. Emphasize the sense of empowerment and freedom that Velocity Banking has brought into your life, as these aspects can deeply resonate with individuals who are currently struggling with debt.

Moreover, as you share your success story, it can be valuable to provide practical tips and lessons learned from your Velocity Banking journey. Offer insights into the strategies and tactics that were particularly effective for you, such as optimizing cash flow, leveraging credit wisely, and staying disciplined with your financial plan. By imparting actionable advice based on your own experiences, you can help others navigate their own Velocity Banking endeavors with greater confidence and clarity.

When sharing your Velocity Banking success story, consider leveraging various platforms and mediums to reach a wider audience. Whether it's through social media, personal blogs, podcasts, or local community events, spreading your story across diverse channels can expand its reach and impact. You may also connect with individuals or organizations that specialize in financial education and debt management, offering to share your story as a guest speaker or contributor.

In conclusion, sharing your Velocity Banking success story is a powerful way to contribute to the financial well-being of others and create a ripple effect of positive change. Through concrete details, emotional insights, practical tips, and strategic dissemination, your story can serve as a catalyst for inspiration and empowerment, helping individuals in debt embark on their own journeys towards financial freedom.